FORTES
IN FIDE

CHURCH MILITANT
PRAYER BOOK

IMPRIMATUR: Madisoniae, die VIII Januarii MMXIII, Jacobus Robertus Bartylla, Vicarius Generalis Diocesis Madisonensis.

NIHIL OBSTAT: die VIII Januarii, MMXIII, Timotheus Cavanaugh, Censor Librorum

ISBN: 0615746195
ISBN-13: 978-0615746197

Deus Vult Press
3673 County Road P
Cross Plains, WI 53528

churchmilitant.com

FORTES IN FIDE

CHURCH MILITANT PRAYER BOOK

BY FR. RICHARD M. HEILMAN

CONTENTS

Few souls understand what God
would accomplish in them if they were
to abandon themselves unreservedly
to Him and if they were to allow
His grace to mold them accordingly.

St. Ignatius Loyola

INTRODUCTION

STRONG IN FAITH

As Jesus ascended to His Father in heaven, He assured His disciples, "You will receive POWER when the Holy Spirit comes upon you and you will be My witnesses" (Acts 1:8). God wants us engaged in this mission, but He wants us strong in His supernatural power.

St. Paul wrote: "Finally, be strong in the Lord and in his mighty POWER. Put on the full armor of God, so that you can take your stand against the devil's schemes. For our struggle is not against flesh and blood, but against the rulers, against the authorities, against the powers of this dark world and against the spiritual forces of evil in the heavenly realms" (Eph 6:10-12).

The momentum of evil in our times has been severe, especially the tsunami of secularism. Why? Because, so conditioned by secularism, we foolishly believe we can defeat these spiritual forces of evil by simply relying upon our own natural power.

St. Peter, our first pope, implored us to be *fortes in fide*, strong in faith, because the devil prowls around like a lion, looking for someone to devour (1 Pt 5:8-9). We know that lions size up a herd to isolate the weakest and easiest target. Once we are detached from God and His supernatural grace, we are powerless to defend ourselves from the tactics of the devil.

Instead, we are being summoned to allow God's powerful supernatural grace to surge through us to a waiting world, but *nemo dat quod non habet* (no one gives what he does not have). Don't we know that our Catholic ancestors couldn't imagine going as much as one day without "being in a state of grace?" They understood that, without grace, they were vulnerable to every whim of the devil while powerless to assist those who had lost their way.

These ancestors were the heroes of our faith, the warrior saints who have gone before us. God worked mightily and miraculously through them. Therefore, we must study their ways. How did they remain so well connected to God so that His river of supernatural grace could flow so freely through them? What do these heroes of faith teach us about the supreme spiritual disciplines, the vital daily regimen of prayer?

YOU ARE A COMMISSIONED OFFICER

From the very first days of our membership in the Mystical Body of Christ, we are, in essence, *commissioned officers in the Church Militant.* In other words, the POWER of the Holy Spirit to combat evil and rescue souls proceeds precisely through the three offices of Christ we receive with the anointing of Sacred Chrism in Baptism: Priest, Prophet, and King.

PRIEST

Fr. Robert Barron says "A priest prays for others, intercedes, and performs sacrifices. ... Priests are border walkers. They walk the border between heaven and earth. They are mediators. They're friends of God and friends of the human race. They bring divinity and humanity together. ... It means you must be a person of prayer — intercessory prayer — prayer on behalf of the people of God. It pleases God to channel His providential care precisely through us and through the instrumentality of our prayer."[1]

PROPHET

For Pope Leo XIII, to be a prophet means we are *"born for combat"*: "'To recoil before an enemy, or to keep silence when from all sides such clamors are raised against truth,' he warns, 'is the part of a man either devoid of character or who entertains doubt as to the truth of what he professes to believe.' The only ones who win when Christians stay quiet he says, are the enemies of truth. The silence of Catholics is particularly disturbing because frequently a few bold words would have vanquished the false ideas. 'Christians are,' Leo continues, *'born for combat.'* It is part of their nature to follow Christ by espousing unpopular ideas and by defending the truth at great cost to themselves." [2]

KING

A king is someone who *leads* others to God. A good king is someone who leads by example. A good king is someone who has the courage and strength to go first, not waiting to follow "popular opinion." Pope St. Pius X would use this military term, *shock troops,* to describe the most necessary need of our time. Shock troops (or assault troops) is a military term that refers to infantry formations, along with supporting units, created to lead an attack. The pope was resolute in acknowledging we are in spiritual warfare as he called for an uncommon valor willing to be the tip of the spear, *the vanguard,* warrior saints unafraid "to lead."[3]

GO WEAPONS HOT!

As a Commissioned Officer in the Church Militant, am I imploring God to *supernaturally weaponize* my prayers (priest), words (prophet), and deeds (king) so that "I can do all things through Christ Who gives me strength" (Phil 4:13)? Or am I ignoring His supernatural strength and power and, therefore, firing blanks?

"Go Weapons Hot" is a military command that means to make whatever preparations are necessary so that when you pull the trigger, something happens. In spiritual terms, are we using live ammunition or are we firing blanks? In other words, are we making the preparations necessary to ensure that our efforts to combat evil and rescue souls are ignited by the fire of the Holy Spirit?

What are the preparations necessary so that "something (effective) happens" as we exercise the three offices of Christ in the war "against the principalities and powers ... the evil spirits in the heavenly realms" (Eph 6:10-12)? The word "hot" ("Go Weapons Hot") gives us an excellent acronym for understanding how we are best positioned to receive the free offer of God's supernatural grace:

H.O.T. = **H**umility, **O**bedience, **T**rust.

H.O.T.

Humility: St. Ignatius of Loyola said, "There is no doubt that God will never be wanting to us, provided that He finds in us that humility which makes us worthy of His gifts, the desire of possessing them, and the promptitude to co-operate industriously with the graces He gives us."

Obedience: St. Josemaria Escriva wrote, "The power of obedience! The lake of Gennesareth had denied its fishes to Peter's nets. A whole night in vain. Then, obedient, he lowered his net again to the water and they caught 'a huge number of fish.' Believe me: the miracle is repeated each day."[4]

Trust: St. Alphonsus Liguori taught: "He who trusts himself is lost. He who trusts in God can do all things." The most important aspect of the Devotion of Divine Mercy is the need to trust in God's goodness. Jesus revealed to St. Faustina, *"the vessel with which souls receive abundant graces, and special favors, is confidence!"* The confident, trusting soul is like a lightning rod for God's mercy and grace.

PART ONE

PRAYER: POWERFUL WEAPON

Prayer is our outstanding supernatural resource for fighting the wiles of the enemy. St. Alphonsus said, "Prayer is, beyond doubt, the most powerful weapon the Lord gives us to conquer evil ... but we must really put ourselves into the prayer, it is not enough just to say the words, it must come from the heart. And also prayer needs to be continuous, we must pray no matter what kind of situation we find ourselves in: the warfare we are engaged in is ongoing, so our prayer must be on-going also."

In referring to his *Seven Daily Habits of Holy Apostolic People*, Fr. John McCloskey writes: "These are the principal means to achieve holiness. If you are a person who wants to bring Christ to others through your friendship, these are the instruments by which you *store up the spiritual energy* that will enable you to do so. Apostolic action without the sacraments and a deep solid interior life will in the long run be ineffective. You can be sure that all the saints incorporated in one way or another all of these habits into their daily routine. Your goal is to be like them, contemplatives in the middle of the world."[5]

SEVEN DAILY HABITS

The following are based in large part on Fr. John McCloskey's *Seven Daily Habits of Holy Apostolic People* and include:

1. The Morning Offering
2. Mental Prayer (at least 15 minutes)
3. Spiritual Reading (at least 15 minutes)
4. Holy Mass and Communion
5. The Angelus (at 12 noon and 6 p.m.)
6. The Holy Rosary
7. Examination of Conscience (at night)

Let's consider some key points before we look more closely at each of these seven daily habits:

First, just like someone who is starting a daily exercise program, you don't go out and run several miles on the first day. That would invite failure, and God wants to see you succeed. Take it easy on yourself as you incorporate these habits in your daily routine over time. Consider using the 12-Week Church Militant Boot Camp from the *Church Militant Field Manual* as a very effective way to get your robust interior life up and running.

Second, while gradually implementing these habits, you still want to make a firm commitment, with the help of the Holy Spirit, to make them the priority in your life — more important than meals, sleep, work, and recreation.

Third, St. Basil writes, "The reason why sometimes you have asked and not received is because you have asked amiss, either inconsistently, or lightly, or because you have asked for what was not good for you, or because you have ceased asking."

It is time to set aside the disorderly, "free-styling" way in which most of us have practiced our daily prayer life throughout our lives. The "cult of the casual" has become so pervasive in the world that it has seeped into our faith lives. This lack of discipline has spelled disaster for those who have ever attempted to maintain regular habits of prayer. These habits must be done when we are most alert, during the day, in a place that is silent and without distractions, where it is easy to put ourselves in God's presence and address Him. Schedule your prayer or it will never happen.

Fourth, Father McCloskey points out that "living the seven daily habits is not a zero sum game. You are not losing time but rather, in reality, gaining it. I have never met a person who lived them on a daily basis who became a less productive worker as a result, or a worse spouse, or who had less time for his friends, or could no longer grow in his cultural life. Quite the contrary, God always rewards those who put Him first. Our Lord will multiply our time amazingly as He did with those few loaves and fishes that fed the multitude with plenty left over." [6]

1. Morning Offering: This is a prayer that lets you begin by offering up your entire day for the glory of God. While there are many formulas for this short prayer, I recommend the one on page 22, as this vintage version includes a plea to seek the indulgences offered that day. St. Josemaria Escriva also encourages us to get up on the dot: "Conquer yourself each day from the very first moment, getting up on the dot, at a set time, without granting a single minute to laziness. If with the help of God, you conquer yourself in the moment, you have accomplished a great deal for the rest of the day. It's so discouraging to find yourself beaten in the first skirmish."[7] This is called the "heroic moment" and gives us the physical and spiritual energy throughout the day to stop what we are doing in order to live the other habits. Once your feet hit the ground, speak the words "I will serve!" (or *Serviam*, in Latin).

2. Mental Prayer (15 minutes): This is "face time," the "one thing necessary" *(unum necessarium)* that constitutes the essential foundation for the interior life. This prayer is simply one-on-one direct conversation with Jesus Christ, preferably before the Blessed Sacrament in the tabernacle. A brief description is found on page 26.

3. Spiritual Reading (15 minutes): This refers to the systematic reading of Sacred Scripture known as Lectio Divina (see page 28) as well as the classic understanding of spiritual reading that is devoted to the reading of lives of saints, writings of Doctors and the Fathers of the Church, and other works written by holy people. As St. Josemaria Escriva puts it, "Don't neglect your spiritual reading. Reading has made many saints."[8]

4. Hear Daily Holy Mass and Receive Holy Communion: This is the most important habit of all the seven. As such, it has to be at the very center of our interior life and consequently our day. St. Peter Julian Eymard tells us to "hear Mass daily; it will prosper the whole day. All your duties will be performed the better for it, and your soul will be stronger to bear its daily cross. The Mass is the most holy act of religion; you can do nothing that can give greater glory to God or be more profitable for your soul than to hear Mass both frequently and devoutly. It is the favorite devotion of the saints."

5. Angelus (or Regina Coeli): This is the very ancient Catholic custom that has us stop what we are doing to greet our Blessed Mother for a moment (at 6:00 a.m., 12:00 noon, and 6:00 p.m. daily), as any good child remembers his mother during the day, and to meditate on the Incarnation and Resurrection of our Lord, which give such meaning to our entire existence. The Regina Coeli is said during the Easter season. The Angelus is said during the rest of the year. See page 24 for these prayers.

6. Holy Rosary: As St. Josemaria Escriva puts it, "For those who use their intelligence and their study as a weapon, the Rosary is most effective, because this apparently monotonous way of beseeching Our Lady, as children do their mother, can destroy every seed of vainglory and pride."[9] Father McCloskey reminds us that "by repeating words of love to Mary and offering up each decade for our intentions, we take the shortcut to Jesus, which is to pass through the heart of Mary. He cannot refuse her anything!"[10] Pope Pius IX once said, "Give me an army saying the Rosary and I will conquer the world." See page 38 for step-by-step instructions for praying the Rosary.

7. Nightly Examination of Conscience: Take a few minutes just before bed to review your day asking, "How have I behaved as a child of God?" It's also a great time to look at that "dominant fault" you need to improve upon in order to become a saint. Conclude these few minutes of reflection by praying three Hail Marys for purity and then pray the "Act of Contrition" (page 30).

Morning Offering

O my God, in union with the Immaculate Heart of Mary (if applicable, here kiss your scapular as sign of your consecration to Mary), I offer Thee the Precious Blood of Jesus from all the altars throughout the world, joining with It the offering of my every thought, word, and action of this day. O my Jesus, I desire today to gain every indulgence and merit I can and I offer them, together with myself, to Mary Immaculate, that she may best apply them in the interests of Thy Most Sacred Heart. Precious Blood of Jesus, save us! Immaculate Heart of Mary, pray for us! Sacred Heart of Jesus, have mercy on us!

Be on your guard;
stand firm in the faith;
be men of courage;
be strong.

1 Cor 16:13

Morning Offering (Option 2)

O Jesus, through the Immaculate Heart of Mary, I offer You my prayers, works, joys, and sufferings of this day in union with the Holy Sacrifice of the Mass throughout the world. I offer them for all the intentions of Your Sacred Heart; the salvation of souls, the reparation for sin, the reunion of Christians; and in particular for the intentions of the Holy Father this month.

*If you are what you
should be,
you will set the
whole world ablaze!*

St. Catherine of Sienna

The Angelus

V. The Angel of the Lord declared unto Mary,
R. And she conceived of the Holy Spirit.
Hail Mary ...

V. Behold the handmaid of the Lord,
R. Be it done unto me according to thy word.
Hail Mary ...

V. And the Word was made Flesh,
R. And dwelt among us.
Hail Mary ...

V. Pray for us, O Holy Mother of God,
R. That we may be made worthy of the promises of Christ.

V. Let us pray. Pour forth, we beseech Thee, O Lord, Thy grace into our hearts; that we to whom the incarnation of Christ, Thy Son, was made known by the message of an angel, may, by His passion and cross, be brought to the glory of His resurrection. Through the same Christ our Lord.

All. Amen.

The Regina Coeli

Queen of Heaven rejoice, alleluia:
For He Whom you did merit to bear, alleluia,

Has risen as He said, alleluia.
Pray for us to God, alleluia.

Rejoice and be glad, O Virgin Mary, alleluia.
For the Lord has truly risen, alleluia.

Let us pray: O God, Who gave joy to the world through the resurrection of Thy Son, our Lord Jesus Christ, grant we beseech Thee, that through the intercession of the Virgin Mary, His mother, we may obtain the joys of everlasting life. Through the same Christ our Lord. Amen.

Love consumes us
only in the measure of
our self-surrender.

St. Therese of Lisieux

Mental Prayer

"Mental prayer is the blessed furnace in which souls are inflamed with the love of God. All the saints have become saints by mental prayer." — St. Alphonsus Liguori

Mental prayer is a form of prayer recommended in the Catholic Church whereby one loves God through dialogue, meditating on God's words, and the contemplation of His Face. It is a time of silence focused on God.

"What matters in prayer is not what we do but what God does in us during those moments," said Fr. Jacques Philippe, "The essential act in prayer is, at bottom, to place one's self in God's presence and to remain there ... This presence, which is that of the living God, is active, vivifying. It heals and sanctifies us. We cannot sit before a fire without getting warm."[11]

Of all human activities,
man's listening to God is the
supreme act of his reasoning
and will.

Pope Paul VI

Preparatory Prayer: My Lord and my God, I firmly believe that You are here, that You see me, that You hear me. I adore You with profound reverence; I ask Your pardon for my sins, and the grace to make this time of prayer fruitful. My immaculate Mother, St. Joseph my father and lord, my guardian angel, intercede for me.

Heart Speaks to Heart (*Cor ad Cor Loquitor*): St. Josemaria Escriva described prayer thus: "To pray is to talk with God. But about what? ... About Him, about yourself — joys, sorrows, successes and failures, noble ambitions, daily worries, weaknesses. And acts of thanksgiving and petitions and love and reparation. In a word, to get to know Him and to get to know yourself. To get acquainted!"[12]

Closing prayer: I thank You, my God, for the good resolutions, affections, and inspirations that You have communicated to me in this meditation. I ask Your help to put them into effect. My immaculate Mother, St. Joseph my father and lord, my guardian angel, intercede for me.

Lectio Divina (Divine Reading)

The following explanation of Lectio Divina is reprinted from Fisheaters.com.[13]

Read/Lectio: When we are relaxed and in a contemplative mode, we trace the Sign of the Cross on the book of Scripture, kiss the Cross we traced, and then open it to read. Some may want to focus on Scripture from the daily Mass. We aren't trying to "accomplish a goal" of reading X amount; we read what is easily digested at that time. Whichever selection we choose, we read it with our minds, slowly, gently, coming to an understanding of the words themselves.

Having a solid Catholic commentary helps us approach Scripture with the mind of the Church. We should always keep in mind Peter's admonition that "no prophecy of Scripture is made by private interpretation" (2 Pt 1:20) and that Scripture can be difficult to understand, something "which the unlearned and unstable wrest ... to their own destruction" (2 Pt 3:16).

If you come to a verse you don't understand, or that you understand in a way that is contrary to Catholic teaching, seek traditional Catholic commentary on it. At any rate, in Lectio, we are reading for the literal sense of the words, trying to understand the reality the writer of the text intended to convey.

Meditate/Meditatio: Now we meditate on what we have read, perhaps even reading it again, visualizing it, and listening for the aspect of it that reveals the Divine Mysteries. We want the deeper, spiritual meanings of the words now, in order to understand the deeper reality the Holy Spirit intends to convey by arranging nature and history as He did, thereby inspiring the writer of the text to write as he did.

Prayer/Oratio: We ask God for the grace to be changed by what we have read, to come more fully into being what He wants us to be, and to help us apply the moral sense of the Scripture to our lives.

Contemplation/Contemplatio: We rest in gratitude for God and His Word.

You will not see anyone who is really striving after his advancement who is not given to spiritual reading. And as to him who neglects it, the fact will soon be observed by his progress.

St. Athanasius

Evening Prayers

The following is from the Handbook of Prayers, *edited by Fr. James Socias, as a good set of practices to follow for evening prayer.*[14]

Make a brief examination of conscience before going to bed at night. Two or three minutes will suffice.

Place yourself in the presence of God, recognizing His strength and your weakness. Tell Him: "Lord, if You will, You can make me clean."

Ask your guardian angel for light to acknowledge your defects and virtues: What have I done wrong? What have I done right? What could I have done better?

Examine your conscience with sincerity: Did I often consider that God is my Father? Did I offer Him my work? Did I make good use of my time? Did I pray slowly and with attention? Did I try to make life pleasant for other people? Did I criticize anyone? Was I forgiving? Did I pray and offer some sacrifices for the Church, for the pope, and for those around me? Did I allow myself to be carried away by sensuality? By pride?

Make an Act of Contrition: O my God, I am heartily sorry for having offended Thee and I detest all my sins because I dread the loss of heaven and the pains of hell, but most of all because they offend Thee, my God, Who art all good and deserving of all my love. I firmly resolve, with the help of Thy grace, to sin no more and avoid the near occasions of sin. Amen.

Make a specific resolution for tomorrow: To stay away from certain temptations. To avoid some specific faults. To exert special effort to practice some virtue. To take advantage of occasion for improvement.

Pray three Hail Marys to the Virgin Mary, asking for purity of heart and body.

Love to be real, it must cost
—it must hurt—
it must empty us of self.

Mother Teresa

Daily Prayers

Grace before Meals

Bless us, O Lord, and these Thy gifts, which we are about to receive, from Thy bounty, through Christ our Lord. Amen.

Benedic, Domine, nos et haec tua dona quae de tua largitate sumus sumpturi per Christum Dominum nostrum. Amen.

Grace after Meals

We give Thee thanks for all Thy benefits, Almighty God, Who lives and reigns forever and ever. Amen.

Agimus tibi gratias, omnipotens Deus, pro universis beneficiis tuis, qui vivis et regnas in saecula saeculorum. Amen.

Guardian Angel Prayer

Angel of God, my guardian dear, to whom God's love commits me here, ever this day be at my side, to light and guard, to rule and guide. Amen.

Angele Dei, qui custos es mei, me tibi commissum pietate superna illumina, custodi, rege, et guberna. Amen.

Memorare

Remember, O most gracious Virgin Mary, that never was it known that anyone who fled to thy protection, implored thy help, or sought thine intercession was left unaided. Inspired by this confidence, I fly unto thee, O Virgin of virgins, my mother; to thee do I come, before thee I stand, sinful and sorrowful. O Mother of the Word Incarnate, despise not my petitions, but in thy mercy hear and answer me. Amen.

Memorare, O piisima Virgo Maria, non esse auditum a saeculo, quemquam ad tua currentem praesidia, tua implorantem auxilia, tua petentem suffragia, esse derelictum. Ego tali animatus confidentia ad te, Virgo Virginum, Mater, curro; ad te venio; coram te gemens peccator assisto. Noli, Mater Verbi, verba mea despicere, sed audi propitia et exaudi. Amen.

Sanctify yourself and you will sanctify society.

St. Francis of Assisi

Praying for Others

Secret Weapon Prayer for Conversion

Here is a secret weapon of which many are not aware. Jesus told St. Faustina, "When you say this prayer, with a contrite heart and with faith on behalf of some sinner, I will give him the grace of conversion." This is the prayer:

"O Blood and Water, which gushed forth from the Heart of Jesus as a fount of Mercy for us, I trust in You."

You should pray this prayer at the beginning of your Chaplet of Divine Mercy for your fallen comrade (someone who has lost or is losing their faith). Also, don't be afraid to pray this "secret weapon prayer" repeatedly, in a stealthy way (inaudibly), for the fallen comrade while you may be seated near her/him. Pray with trust.

Since you cannot do good to all,
you are to pay special attention to those
who, by the accidents of time, or place,
or circumstances, are brought into
closer connection with you.

St. Augustine

Sacred Heart Novena Prayer

When someone asks you to pray for them, use the prayer below (by St. Margaret Mary Alacoque) which Padre Pio would use when people asked him to pray for them.

O my Jesus, You have said: "Truly I say to you, ask and you will receive, seek and you will find, knock and it will be opened to you." Behold I knock, I seek and ask for the grace of (here name your request). Our Father ... Hail Mary ... Glory Be ... Sacred Heart of Jesus, I place all my trust in You.

O my Jesus, You have said: "Truly I say to you, if you ask anything of the Father in My name, He will give it to you." Behold, in Your name, I ask the Father for the grace of (here name your request). Our Father ... Hail Mary ... Glory Be ... Sacred Heart of Jesus, I place all my trust in You.

O my Jesus, You have said: "Truly I say to you, heaven and earth will pass away but My words will not pass away." Encouraged by Your infallible words I now ask for the grace of (here name your request). Our Father ... Hail Mary ... Glory Be ... Sacred Heart of Jesus, I place all my trust in You.

O Sacred Heart of Jesus, for whom it is impossible not to have compassion on the afflicted, have pity on us miserable sinners and grant us the grace which we ask of You, through the Sorrowful and Immaculate Heart of Mary, Your tender Mother and ours.

Say the Hail, Holy Queen (page 43) and add: "St. Joseph, foster father of Jesus, pray for us."

Prayer for Healing the Family Tree

Heavenly Father, I come before You as Your child, in great need of Your help; I have physical health needs, emotional needs, spiritual needs, and interpersonal needs. Many of my problems have been caused by my own failures, neglect, and sinfulness, for which I humbly beg Your forgiveness, Lord. But I also ask You to forgive the sins of my ancestors whose failures have left their effects on me in the form of unwanted tendencies, behavior patterns, and defects in body, mind, and spirit. Heal me, Lord, of all these disorders.

With Your help I sincerely forgive everyone, especially living or dead members of my family tree, who have directly offended me or my loved ones in any way, or those whose sins have resulted in our present sufferings and disorders. In the name of Your divine Son, Jesus, and in the power of His Holy Spirit, I ask You, Father, to deliver me and my entire family tree from the influence of the evil one. Free all living and dead members of my family tree, including those in adoptive relationships and those in extended family relationships, from every contaminating form of bondage. By Your loving concern for us, heavenly Father, and by the shed blood of Your precious Son, Jesus, I beg You to extend Your blessing to me and to all my living and deceased relatives. Heal every negative effect transmitted through all past generations, and prevent such negative effects in future generations of my family tree.

I symbolically place the cross of Jesus over the head of each person in my family tree and between each generation; I ask You to let the cleansing blood of Jesus purify the bloodlines in my family lineage. Set Your protective angels to encamp around us, and permit Archangel Raphael, the patron of healing, to administer Your divine healing power to all of us, even in areas of genetic disability. Give special power to our family members' guardian angels to heal, protect, guide, and encourage each of us in all our needs. Let Your healing power be released at this very moment, and let it continue as long as Your sovereignty permits.

In our family tree, Lord, replace all bondage with a holy bonding in family love. And let there be an ever-deeper bonding with You, Lord, by the Holy Spirit, to Your Son, Jesus. Let the family of the Holy Trinity pervade our family with its tender, warm, loving presence, so that our family may recognize and manifest that love in all our relationships. All of our unknown needs we include with this petition that we pray in Jesus' precious Name. Amen.

St. Joseph, patron of family life, pray for us.

By Fr. John Hampsch

Holy Rosary

How to pray the Rosary:

1. Make the Sign of the Cross; pray the Apostles' Creed (while holding the crucifix).
2. Pray the Our Father (on the first large bead).
3. Pray 3 Hail Marys (on each of the 3 small beads).
4. Pray the Glory Be.
5. Announce the first mystery, then pray the Our Father (on the large bead).
6. Pray 10 Hail Marys while meditating on the mystery (on each of the next 10 beads).
7. Pray the Glory Be followed by the Fatima Prayer.
8. Repeat steps 5, 6, and 7 for the remaining mysteries.
9. Pray the Hail, Holy Queen after the five decades are completed.
10. Pray the optional closing prayer; to gain the indulgence, pray an Our Father and a Hail Mary for the pope's intentions; make the Sign of the Cross.

Optional Closing Prayer for the Rosary:

V. Let us pray,
R. O God, Whose only begotten Son, by His life, death, and resurrection, has purchased for us the rewards of eternal salvation, grant, we beseech Thee, that while meditating on these mysteries of the most holy Rosary of the Blessed Virgin Mary, we may imitate what they contain and obtain what they promise, through Christ our Lord. Amen.

Mysteries and Fruits of the Holy Rosary

The Joyful Mysteries (Monday, Saturday)
1. The Annunciation — Humility
2. The Visitation — Charity
3. Nativity of the Lord — Detachment from World
4. Presentation — Purity
5. Finding of the Child Jesus in the Temple —
   Obedience to the Will of God

Sorrowful Mysteries (Tuesday, Friday)
1. Agony in the Garden — Resignation to Will of God
2. Scourging at the Pillar — Mortification
3. Crowning with Thorns — Moral Courage
4. Carrying of the Cross — Patience in Adversity
5. Crucifixion — Love of Enemies

Glorious Mysteries (Wednesday, Sunday)
1. The Resurrection — Faith
2. The Ascension — Hope
3. The Descent of the Holy Spirit — Love of God
4. The Assumption of Mary — Devotion to Mary
5. The Coronation of the Blessed Virgin Mary —
   Eternal Happiness

The Luminous Mysteries (Thursday)
1. Baptism of Jesus — Openness to the Holy Spirit
2. The Miracle at Cana — To Jesus through Mary
3. Proclamation of the Kingdom of God —
   Repentance, Trust in God
4. Transfiguration — Desire for Holiness
5. Institution of the Eucharist — Eucharistic
   Adoration

Sign of the Cross

In the Name of the Father and of the Son and of the Holy Spirit. Amen.

In nomine Patris, et Filii, et Spiritus Sancti. Amen.

Apostles' Creed

I believe in God, the Father almighty, Creator of heaven and earth, and in Jesus Christ, His only Son, our Lord, Who was conceived by the Holy Spirit, born of the Virgin Mary, suffered under Pontius Pilate, was crucified, died, and was buried; He descended into hell; on the third day He rose again from the dead; He ascended into heaven, and is seated at the right hand of God the Father almighty; from there He will come to judge the living and the dead. I believe in the Holy Spirit, the holy catholic Church, the communion of saints, the forgiveness of sins, the resurrection of the body, and life everlasting. Amen.

Credo in Deum Patrem omnipotentem, Creatorem caeli et terrae. Et in Iesum Christum, Filium eius unicum, Dominum nostrum, qui conceptus est de Spiritu Sancto, natus ex Maria Virgine, passus sub Pontio Pilato, crucifixus, mortuus, et sepultus, descendit ad infernos, tertia die resurrexit a mortuis, ascendit ad caelos, sedet ad dexteram Dei Patris omnipotentis, inde venturus est iudicare vivos et mortuos. Credo in Spiritum Sanctum, sanctam Ecclesiam catholicam, sanctorum communionem, remissionem peccatorum, carnis resurrectionem, vitam aeternam. Amen.

Our Father

Our Father, Who art in heaven, hallowed be Thy name. Thy kingdom come; Thy will be done on earth, as it is in heaven. Give us this day our daily bread, and forgive us our trespasses, as we forgive those who trespass against us. And lead us not into temptation, but deliver us from evil. Amen.

Pater noster, qui es in caelis, sanctificetur nomen tuum. Adveniat regnum tuum. Fiat voluntas tua, sicut in caelo et in terra. Panem nostrum quotidianum da nobis hodie, et dimitte nobis debita nostra sicut et nos dimittimus debitoribus nostris. Et ne nos inducas in tentationem, sed libera nos a malo. Amen.

Hail Mary

Hail Mary, full of grace; the Lord is with thee; blessed art thou among women, and blessed is the fruit of thy womb, Jesus. Holy Mary, Mother of God, pray for us sinners, now and at the hour of our death. Amen.

Ave Maria, gratia plena, Dominus tecum. Benedicta tu in mulieribus, et benedictus fructus ventris tui, Iesus. Sancta Maria, Mater Dei, ora pro nobis peccatoribus, nunc, et in hora mortis nostrae. Amen.

Glory Be

Glory be to the Father, and to the Son, and to the Holy Spirit. As it was in the beginning, is now, and will be forever. Amen.

Gloria Patri, et Filio, et Spiritui Sancto. Sicut erat in principio, et nunc, et semper, et in saecula saeculorum. Amen.

Fatima Prayer

O my Jesus, forgive us our sins; save us from the fires of hell. Lead all souls to heaven, especially those who are most in need of Your mercy.

Domine Iesu, dimitte nobis debita nostra, salva nos ab igne inferiori, perduc in caelum omnes animas, praesertim eas, quae misericordiae tuae maxime indigent.

> God gives each one of us sufficient grace ever to know His holy will, and to do it fully.
>
> *St. Ignatius of Loyola*

Hail, Holy Queen

Hail, holy Queen, Mother of Mercy; our life, our sweetness, and our hope. To thee do we cry, poor banished children of Eve; to thee do we send up our sighs, mourning and weeping in this valley of tears. Turn, then, most gracious advocate, thine eyes of mercy towards us; and after this our exile, show unto us the blessed fruit of thy womb, Jesus. O clement, O loving, O sweet Virgin Mary.

V. Pray for us, O holy Mother of God.

R. That we may be made worthy of the promises of Christ.

Salve Regina, Mater misericordiae. Vita, dulcedo, et spes nostra, salve. Ad te clamamus exsules filii Hevae. Ad te suspiramus, gementes et flentes in hac lacrimarum valle. Eia ergo, Advocata nostra, illos tuos misericordes oculos ad nos converte. Et Iesum, benedictum fructum ventris tui, nobis post hoc exsilium ostende. O clemens, O pia, O dulcis Virgo Maria.

V. Ora pro nobis, Sancta Dei Genitrix.

R. Ut digni efficiamur promissionibus Christi.

Chaplet of Divine Mercy

1. Make the Sign of the Cross.

2. Opening prayers (optional):

You expired, Jesus, but the source of life gushed forth for souls, and the ocean of mercy opened up for the whole world. O Fount of Life, unfathomable Divine Mercy, envelop the whole world and empty Yourself out upon us.

O Blood and Water, which gushed forth from the Heart of Jesus as a fountain of mercy for us, I trust in You! (Repeat three times.)

3. Say an Our Father, a Hail Mary, and the Apostle's Creed (on the three small beads).

4. Pray an Eternal Father (on the large bead):

Eternal Father, I offer You the Body and Blood, Soul and Divinity of Your Dearly Beloved Son, Our Lord, Jesus Christ, in atonement for our sins and those of the whole world.

5. On each of the 10 "Hail Mary" beads pray:

For the sake of His sorrowful Passion, have mercy on us and on the whole world.

6. For the remaining decades, repeat #4 and #5.

7. Conclude by repeating three times:

Holy God, Holy Mighty One, Holy Immortal One, have mercy on us and on the whole world.

8. Say the closing prayers (optional):

Eternal God, in Whom mercy is endless and the treasury of compassion inexhaustible, look kindly upon us and increase Your mercy in us, that in difficult moments we might not despair nor become despondent, but with great confidence submit ourselves to Your holy will, which is Love and Mercy itself.

It is not the actual physical exertion
that counts towards a man's progress,
nor the nature of the task,
but the spirit of faith with
which it is undertaken.

St. Francis Xavier

Prayers for Mass

Before Mass

Prayer of St. Ambrose

Lord Jesus Christ, I approach Thy banquet table in fear and trembling, for I am a sinner, and dare not rely on my own worth, but only on Thy goodness and mercy. I am defiled by my many sins in body and soul, and by my unguarded thoughts and words. Gracious God of majesty and awe, I seek Thy protection, I look for Thy healing. Poor troubled sinner that I am, I appeal to Thee, the fountain of all mercy. I cannot bear Thy judgment, but I trust in Thy salvation. Lord, I show my wounds to Thee and uncover my shame before Thee. I know my sins are many and great, and they fill me with fear, but I hope in Thy mercies, for they cannot be numbered. Lord Jesus Christ, Eternal King, God and man, crucified for mankind, look upon me with mercy and hear my prayer, for I trust in Thee. Have mercy on me, full of sorrow and sin, for the depth of Thy compassion never ends. Praise to Thee, Saving Sacrifice, offered on the wood of the cross for me and for all mankind. Praise to the noble and precious Blood, flowing from the wounds of my crucified Lord Jesus Christ and washing away the sins of the whole world. Remember, Lord, Thy creature, whom Thou hast redeemed with Thy blood; I repent my sins, and I long to put right what I have done.

Merciful Father, take away all my offenses and sins; purify me in body and soul, and make me worthy to taste the Holy of Holies. May Thy Body and Blood, which I intend to receive, although I am unworthy, be for me the remission of my sins, the washing away of my guilt, the end of my evil thoughts, and the rebirth of my better instincts. May it incite me to do the works pleasing to Thee and profitable to my health in body and soul, and be a firm defense against the wiles of my enemies. Amen.

Prayer of St. Thomas Aquinas

Almighty and ever-living God, I approach the sacrament of Thy only-begotten Son, our Lord Jesus Christ. I come sick to the Doctor of life, unclean to the Fountain of mercy, blind to the Radiance of eternal light, and poor and needy to the Lord of heaven and earth. Lord, in Thy great generosity, heal my sickness, wash away my defilement, enlighten my blindness, enrich my poverty, and clothe my nakedness. May I receive the Bread of Angels, the King of kings and the Lord of lords, with humble reverence, with the purity and faith, the repentance and love, and the determined purpose that will help to bring me to salvation. May I receive the sacrament of the Lord's body and blood, in its reality and power. Kind God, may I receive the Body of Thy only-begotten Son, our Lord Jesus Christ, born from the womb of the Virgin Mary, and so be received into His mystical body, and numbered among His members. Loving Father, as on my earthly pilgrimage I now receive Thy beloved Son under the veil of a sacrament, may I one day see Him face to face in glory, Who lives and reigns with Thee in the unity of the Holy Spirit, God, forever. Amen.

Prayer to All the Angels and Saints

Angels, archangels, thrones, dominations, principalities, powers, heavenly virtues, cherubim and seraphim, all saints of God, holy men and women, and you especially my patrons: deign to intercede for me that I may be worthy to offer this sacrifice to almighty God, to the praise and glory of His name, for my own welfare and also that of all His holy Church. Amen.

This very moment I may, if I desire, become the friend of God.

St. Augustine

Before Communion

Prayer of St. Anselm

O Lord Jesus Christ, Son of the Living God, Who according to the will of the Father and with the cooperation of the Holy Spirit hast by Thy death given life unto the world, I adore and revere this Thy holy Body and this Thy holy Blood which was given over and poured forth for the many unto the remission of sins. O merciful Lord, I beg of Thy mercy that through the power of this sacrament Thou willst make me one of that many. Through faith and love make me feel the power of these sacraments so I may experience their saving power. Absolve and free from all sin and punishment of sin Thy servants, Thy handmaidens, myself, all who have confessed their sins to me, those whom I have promised or am obliged to pray for, and so too those who themselves hope or beg to be helped by my prayers with Thee. Make our Church rejoice in Thy constant protection and consolation. Amen.

Golden Arrow Prayer

May the most holy, most sacred, most adorable, most incomprehensible and unutterable Name of God be always praised, blessed, loved, adored, and glorified in heaven, on earth, and under the earth, by all the creatures of God and by the Sacred Heart of Our Lord Jesus Christ, in the Most Holy Sacrament of the Altar. Amen.

After Communion

Anima Christi

Soul of Christ, sanctify me. Body of Christ, save me. Blood of Christ, inebriate me. Water from the side of Christ, wash me. Passion of Christ, strengthen me. O good Jesus, hear me. Within thy wounds, hide me. Permit me not to be separated from Thee. From the wicked foe, defend me. At the hour of my death, call me. And bid me come to Thee. That with all Thy saints, I may praise Thee Forever and ever. Amen.

Prayer of St. Ignatius of Loyola

Lord Jesus Christ, take all my freedom, my memory, my understanding, and my will. All that I have and cherish Thou hast given me. I surrender it all to be guided by Thy will. Thy grace and Thy love are wealth enough for me. Give me these Lord Jesus and I ask for nothing more. Amen.

Prayer of St. Bonaventure

Pierce, O most sweet Lord Jesus, my inmost soul with the most joyous and healthful wound of Thy love, with true, serene, and most holy apostolic charity, that my soul may ever languish and melt with love and longing for Thee, that it may yearn for Thee and faint for Thy courts, and long to be dissolved and to be with Thee. Grant that my soul may hunger after Thee, the bread of angels, the refreshment of holy souls, our daily and supersubstantial bread, having all sweetness and savor and every delight of taste; let my heart ever hunger after and feed upon Thee, upon Whom the angels desire to look, and may my inmost soul be filled with the sweetness of Thy savor; may it ever thirst after Thee, the fountain of life, the fountain of wisdom and knowledge, the fountain of eternal light, the torrent of pleasure, the richness of the house of God. May it ever compass Thee, seek Thee, find Thee, run to Thee, attain Thee, meditate upon Thee, speak of Thee, and do all things to the praise and glory of Thy name, with humility and discretion, with love and delight, with ease and affection, and with perseverance unto the end; may Thou alone be ever my hope, my entire assurance, my riches, my delight, my pleasure, my joy, my rest and tranquility, my peace, my sweetness, my fragrance, my sweet savor, my food, my refreshment, my refuge, my help, my wisdom, my portion, my possession, and my treasure, in Whom may my mind and my heart be fixed and firmly rooted immovably henceforth and forever. Amen.

Prayer of St. Thomas Aquinas

I thank You, O holy Lord, almighty Father, eternal God, Who have deigned, not through any merits of mine, but out of the condescension of Your goodness, to satisfy me a sinner, Your unworthy servant, with the precious Body and Blood of Your Son, our Lord Jesus Christ.

I pray that this Holy Communion be not a condemnation to punishment for me, but a saving plea to forgiveness.

May it be to me the armor of faith and the shield of a good will.

May it be the emptying out of my vices and the extinction of all lustful desires; an increase of charity and patience, of humility and obedience, and all virtues; a strong defense against the snares of all my enemies, visible and invisible; the perfect quieting of all my evil impulses of flesh and spirit, binding me firmly to You, the one true God; and a happy ending of my life.

I pray too that You will deign to bring me, a sinner, to that ineffable banquet where You with Your Son and the Holy Spirit, are to Your saints true light, fulfillment of desires, eternal joy, unalloyed gladness, and perfect bliss. Through the same Christ our Lord. Amen.

Come, Holy Spirit

Come, Holy Spirit, fill the hearts of Thy faithful and enkindle in them the fire of Thy love.

V. Send forth Thy Spirit and they shall be created.

R. And Thou shalt renew the face of the earth.

Let us pray. O God, Who didst instruct the hearts of the faithful by the light of the Holy Spirit, grant us in the same Spirit to be truly wise, and ever to rejoice in His consolation. Through Christ our Lord. Amen.

Litany of Humility

O Jesus meek and humble of heart, Hear me.
From the desire of being esteemed, Deliver me, Jesus.
From the desire of being loved, Deliver me, Jesus.
From the desire of being extolled, Deliver me, Jesus.
From the desire of being honored, Deliver me, Jesus.
From the desire of being praised, Deliver me, Jesus.
From the desire of being preferred to others, Deliver me, Jesus.
From the desire of being consulted, Deliver me, Jesus.
From the desire of being approved, Deliver me, Jesus.
From the fear of being humiliated, Deliver me, Jesus.
From the fear of being despised, Deliver me, Jesus.

From the fear of suffering rebukes, Deliver me, Jesus.

From the fear of being calumniated, Deliver me, Jesus.

From the fear of being forgotten, Deliver me, Jesus.

From the fear of being ridiculed, Deliver me, Jesus.

From the fear of being wronged, Deliver me, Jesus.

From the fear of being suspected, Deliver me, Jesus.

That others may be loved more than I, Jesus, grant me the grace to desire it.

That others may be esteemed more than I, Jesus, grant me the grace to desire it.

That in the opinion of the world, others may increase, and I may decrease, Jesus, grant me the grace to desire it.

That others may be chosen and I set aside, Jesus, grant me the grace to desire it.

That others may be praised and I unnoticed, Jesus, grant me the grace to desire it.

That others may be preferred to me in everything, Jesus, grant me the grace to desire it.

That others may become holier than I, provided that I become as holy as I should, Jesus, grant me the grace to desire it.

Prayer of Padre Pio

Stay with me, Lord, for it is necessary to have You present so that I do not forget You. You know how easily I abandon You.

Stay with me, Lord, because I am weak and I need Your strength, that I may not fall so often.

Stay with me, Lord, for You are my life, and without You, I am without fervor.

Stay with me, Lord, for You are my light, and without You, I am in darkness.

Stay with me, Lord, to show me Your will.

Stay with me, Lord, so that I hear Your voice and follow You.

Stay with me, Lord, for I desire to love You very much, and always be in Your company.

Stay with me, Lord, if You wish me to be faithful to You.

Stay with me, Lord, for as poor as my soul is, I wish it to be a place of consolation for You, a nest of Love.

Stay with me, Jesus, for it is getting late and the day is coming to a close, and life passes; death, judgment, eternity approaches. It is necessary to renew my strength, so that I will not stop along the way, and for that, I need You. It is getting late and death approaches. I fear the darkness, the temptations, the dryness, the cross, the sorrows. O how I need You, my Jesus, in this night of exile!

Stay with me tonight, Jesus, in life with all its dangers, I need You.

Let me recognize You as Your disciples did at the breaking of bread, so that the Eucharistic Communion be the light which disperses the darkness, the force which sustains me, the unique joy of my heart.

Stay with me, Lord, because at the hour of my death, I want to remain united to You, if not by Communion, at least by grace and love.

Stay with me, Jesus, I do not ask for divine consolation, because I do not merit it, but, the gift of Your Presence, oh yes, I ask this of You!

Stay with me, Lord, for it is You alone I look for, Your Love, Your Grace, Your Will, Your Heart, Your Spirit, because I love You and ask no other reward but to love You more and more.

With a firm love, I will love You with all my heart while on earth and continue to love You perfectly during all eternity. Amen.

Pray, hope, and don't worry.

St. Padre Pio

After Mass

Prayer to St. Michael the Archangel

St. Michael the Archangel, defend us in battle; be our defense against the wickedness and snares of the devil. May God rebuke him, we humbly pray. And do thou, O prince of the heavenly host, by the power of God, thrust into hell Satan and all the evil spirits who prowl about the world seeking the ruin of souls. Amen.

Hear Mass daily; it will prosper
the whole day. All your duties will
be performed the better for it,
and your soul will be stronger
to bear its daily cross.
The Mass is the most holy act
of religion; you can do nothing
that can give greater glory to God
or be more profitable for your soul
than to hear Mass both
frequently and devoutly.
It is the favorite devotion of the saints.

St. Peter Julian Eymard

Prayers before the Blessed Sacrament

O Salutaris (by St. Thomas Aquinas):

O salutaris Hostia, Quae caeli pandis ostium: Bella premunt hostilia, Da robur, fer auxilium.

Uni trinoque Domino Sit sempiterna gloria, Qui vitam sine termino Nobis donet in patria. Amen.

O saving Victim, opening wide, the gate of heaven to man below! Our foes press on from every side; Thine aid supply, Thy strength bestow.

To Thy great name be endless praise, Immortal Godhead, One in Three; Oh, grant us endless length of days, in our true native land with Thee. Amen.

Tantum Ergo (by St. Thomas Aquinas):

Tantum ergo Sacramentum Veneremur cernui: Et antiquum documentum Novo cedat ritui: Praestet fides supplementum Sensuum defectui.

Genitori, Genitoque Laus et jubilatio, Salus, honor, virtus quoque Sit et benedictio: Procedenti ab utroque Compar sit laudatio. Amen.

Down in adoration falling, Lo! the sacred Host we hail, Lo! o'er ancient forms departing, newer rites of grace prevail; Faith for all defects supplying, where the feeble senses fail.

To the everlasting Father, and the Son Who reigns on high, with the Holy Spirit proceeding, forth from each eternally, be salvation, honor, blessing, might, and endless majesty. Amen.

Prayer of St. Alphonsus Liguori

To begin visit:

My Lord Jesus Christ, Who because of Your love for men remain night and day in the Blessed Sacrament, full of pity and of love, awaiting, calling, and welcoming all who come to visit You, I believe that You are present here on the altar. I adore You, and I thank You for all the graces You have bestowed on me, especially for having given me Yourself in this sacrament, for having given me Your most holy Mother Mary to plead for me, and for having called me to visit You in this church.

I now salute Your most loving Heart, and that for three ends: first, in thanksgiving for this great gift; secondly, to make amends to You for all the outrages committed against You in this sacrament by Your enemies; thirdly, I intend by this visit to adore You in all the places on earth in which You are present in the Blessed Sacrament and in which You are least honored and most abandoned.

My Jesus, I love You with my whole heart. I am very sorry for having so many times offended Your infinite goodness. With the help of Your grace, I purpose never to offend You again. And now, unworthy though I am, I consecrate myself to You without reserve. I renounce and give entirely to You my will, my affection, my desires, and all that I possess. For the future, dispose of me and all I have as You please.

All I ask of You is Your holy love, final perseverance, and that I may carry out Your will perfectly. I recommend to You the souls in purgatory, especially those who had the greatest devotion to the Blessed Sacrament and to the Blessed Virgin Mary. I also recommend to You all poor sinners.

Finally, my dear Savior, I unite all my desires with the desires of Your most loving Heart; and I offer them, thus united, to the Eternal Father, and beseech Him, in Your name and for love of You, to accept and grant them.

Prayer of St. Alphonsus Liguori

To conclude visit:

Most holy Virgin Immaculate, my Mother Mary, it is to you, who are the Mother of my Lord, the Queen of the world, the advocate, the hope, and the refuge of sinners, that I have recourse today, I, who most of all am deserving of pity. Most humbly do I offer you my homage, O great Queen, and I thank you for all the graces you have obtained for me until now, and particularly for having saved me from hell, which, by my sins, I have so often deserved.

I love you, O most lovable Lady, and because of my love for you, I promise to serve you always and to do all in my power to win others to love you also. In your hands I place all my hopes; I entrust the salvation of my soul to your care. Accept me as your servant, O Mother of Mercy; receive me under your mantle. And since you have such power with God, deliver me from all temptations, or rather, obtain for me the strength to triumph over them until death. Of you I ask the grace of perfect love for Jesus Christ. Through your help I hope to die a happy death. O my Mother I beg you, by the love you bear my God, to help me at all times, but especially at the last moment of my life. Do not leave me, I beseech you, until you see me safe in heaven, blessing you and singing your mercies for all eternity. Amen, so I hope, so may it be.

He who trusts himself is lost.
He who trusts in God
can do all things.

St. Alphonsus Liguori

Divine Praises

Blessed be God.

Blessed be His Holy Name.

Blessed be Jesus Christ, true God and true man.

Blessed be the name of Jesus.

Blessed be His Most Sacred Heart.

Blessed be His Most Precious Blood.

Blessed be Jesus in the Most Holy Sacrament of the Altar.

Blessed be the Holy Spirit, the Paraclete.

Blessed be the great Mother of God, Mary most holy.

Blessed be her holy and Immaculate Conception.

Blessed be her glorious Assumption.

Blessed be the name of Mary, Virgin and Mother.

Blessed be Saint Joseph, her most chaste spouse.

Blessed be God in His angels and in His Saints.

*It is not hard to obey
when we love the one whom we obey.*

St. Ignatius of Loyola

Spiritual Communion

(For when you are unable to attend Mass or receive Communion.)

My Jesus, I believe that Thou art present in the Blessed Sacrament. I love Thee above all things and I desire Thee in my soul. Since I cannot now receive Thee sacramentally, come at least spiritually into my heart. As though Thou wert already there, I embrace Thee and unite myself wholly to Thee; permit not that I should ever be separated from Thee. Amen.

To one who has faith,
no explanation is necessary.
To one without faith,
no explanation is possible.

St. Thomas Aquinas

Manner of Making Confession

(Having entered the confessional, place yourself in the presence of God, Who sees all things, and then address His minister):

Bless me, Father, for I have sinned.

I confess to almighty God, and to you, Father, that I have sinned exceedingly in thought, word, deed, and omission, through my fault.

It has been ___ weeks since my last Confession. I accuse myself of having committed, during that time, the following sins:

(State your sins here)

For these, and all the sins of which I have at any time been guilty, I humbly ask pardon of God, and absolution of you, Father, if you think me worthy.

(Then listen intently to anything the confessor may choose to say; humbly accept the penance he imposes, and, once he has completed the prayer of absolution, recite the act of contrition.)

The Act of Contrition:

O My God, I am heartily sorry for having offended Thee and I detest all my sins because I dread the loss of heaven and the pains of hell, but most of all because they offend Thee, my God, Who art all good and deserving of all my love. I firmly resolve, with the help of Thy grace, to sin no more and avoid the near occasions of sin. Amen.

(After Confession we should return thanks to God for His mercies in forgiving our sins, beg that He supply whatever has been wanting in us and bless our good resolutions, and immediately thereafter say our penance.)

Let us therefore give ourselves
to God with a great desire to
begin to live thus,
and beg Him to destroy in us the
life of the world of sin,
and to establish His life within us.

St. John Eudes

Examination of Conscience

Special thanks to Beginning Catholic *for this examination.*[15]

To make an examination:
✠ Set aside some quiet time for reflection.
✠ Start by praying to the Holy Spirit, asking for help in making a good examination to prepare for Confession.
✠ Read through the items on this list and honestly reflect on your behavior for each item.
✠ If necessary, take this list or brief notes (keep them private!) to Confession to help you remember things.

First Commandment:
You shall worship the Lord your God and Him only shall you serve. Have I ...
✠ Disobeyed the commandments of God or the Church?
✠ Refused to accept what God has revealed as true, or what the Catholic Church proposes for belief?
✠ Denied the existence of God?
✠ Failed to nourish and protect my faith?
✠ Rejected everything opposed to a sound faith?
✠ Deliberately misled others about doctrine or the faith?

✠ Rejected the Catholic faith, joined another Christian denomination, or joined or practiced another religion?

✠ Joined a group forbidden to Catholics (Masons, communists, etc.)?

✠ Despaired about my salvation or the forgiveness of my sins?

✠ Presumed on God's mercy? (Committing a sin in expectation of forgiveness, or asking for forgiveness without conversion and practicing virtue.)

✠ Loved someone or something more than God (money, power, sex, ambition, etc.)?

✠ Let someone or something influence my choices more than God?

✠ Engaged in superstitious practices? (Including horoscopes, fortunetellers, etc.)

✠ Been involved in the occult? (séances, Ouija board, worship of Satan, etc.)

✠ Formally left the Catholic Church?

✠ Hidden a serious sin or told a lie in Confession?

Second Commandment

You shall not take the name of the Lord your God in vain. Have I...

✠ Used the name of God in cursing or blasphemy?

✠ Failed to keep vows or promises that I have made to God?

✠ Spoken about the faith, the Church, the saints, or sacred things with irreverence, hatred, or defiance?

✠ Watched television or movies or listened to music that treated God, the Church, the saints, or sacred things irreverently?

✠ Used vulgar, suggestive, or obscene speech?

✠ Belittled others in my speech?

✠ Behaved disrespectfully in Church?

✠ Misused places or things set apart for the worship of God?

✠ Committed perjury? (Breaking an oath or lying under oath.)

✠ Blamed God for my failings?

Third Commandment
Remember to keep holy the Sabbath day. Have I ...

✠ Set time aside each day for personal prayer to God?

✠ Missed Mass on Sunday or Holy Days (through my own fault without sufficient reason)?

✠ Committed a sacrilege against the Blessed Sacrament?

✠ Received a sacrament while in the state of mortal sin?

✠ Habitually came late to and/or left early from Mass without a good reason?

✠ Shopped, labored, or done business unnecessarily on Sunday or other Holy Days of Obligation?

✠ Not attended to taking my children to Mass?

✠ Knowingly eaten meat on a day of abstinence (or not fasted on a fast day)?

✠ Eaten or drank within one hour of receiving Communion (other than water or medical need)?

Fourth Commandment

Honor your father and your mother. Have I ...

✠ Obeyed all that my parents reasonably asked of me? (If still under my parents' care.)

✠ Neglected the needs of my parents in their old age or in their time of need?

✠ Obeyed the reasonable demands of my teachers? (If still in school.)

✠ Neglected to give my children proper food, clothing, shelter, education, discipline, and care (even after Confirmation)?

✠ Provided for the religious education and formation of my children for as long as they were under my care?

✠ Ensured that my children still under my care regularly frequent the sacraments of Penance and Holy Communion?

✠ Educated my children in a way that corresponds to my religious convictions?

✠ Provided my children with a positive, prudent, and personalized education in the Catholic teaching on human sexuality?

✠ Been to my children a good example of how to live the Catholic faith?

✠ Prayed with and for my children?

✠ Lived in humble obedience to those who legitimately exercise authority over me?

✠ Broken the law?

✠ Supported or voted for a politician whose positions are opposed to the teachings of Christ and the Catholic Church?

Fifth Commandment
You shall not kill. Have I ...

✠ Unjustly and intentionally killed a human being?
✠ Been involved in an abortion, directly or indirectly (through advice, etc.)?
✠ Seriously considered or attempted suicide?
✠ Supported, promoted, or encouraged the practice of assisted suicide or mercy killing?
✠ Deliberately desired to kill an innocent human being?
✠ Unjustly inflicted bodily harm on another person?
✠ Unjustly threatened another person with bodily harm?
✠ Verbally or emotionally abused another person?
✠ Hated another person, or wished him evil?
✠ Been prejudiced or unjustly discriminating against others because of their race, color, nationality, sex, or religion?
✠ Joined a hate group?
✠ Purposely provoked another by teasing or nagging?
✠ Recklessly endangered my life or health, or that of another, by my actions?
✠ Driven recklessly or under the influence of alcohol or other drugs?
✠ Abused alcohol or other drugs?
✠ Sold or given drugs to others to use for non-therapeutic purposes?
✠ Used tobacco immoderately?
✠ Over-eaten?

- ✠ Encouraged others to sin by giving scandal?
- ✠ Helped another to commit a mortal sin? (through advice, driving them somewhere, etc.)
- ✠ Caused serious injury or death by criminal neglect?
- ✠ Indulged in serious anger?
- ✠ Refused to control my temper?
- ✠ Been mean to, quarreled with, or willfully hurt someone?
- ✠ Been unforgiving to others, when mercy or pardon was requested?
- ✠ Sought revenge or hoped something bad would happen to someone?
- ✠ Delighted to see someone else get hurt or suffer?
- ✠ Treated animals cruelly, causing them to suffer or die needlessly?

Sixth and Ninth Commandments
You shall not commit adultery. You shall not covet your neighbor's wife. Have I ...

✠ Practiced the virtue of chastity?

✠ Given in to lust? (The desire for sexual pleasure unrelated to spousal love in marriage.)

✠ Used an artificial means of birth control?

✠ Refused to be open to conception, without just cause? (Catechism of the Catholic Church paragraph 2368)

✠ Participated in immoral techniques for in vitro fertilization or artificial insemination?

✠ Sterilized my sex organs for contraceptive purposes?

✠ Deprived my spouse of the marital right, without just cause?

✠ Claimed my own marital right without concern for my spouse?

✠ Deliberately caused climax outside of normal sexual intercourse? (Catechism of the Catholic Church paragraph 2366)

✠ Willfully entertained impure thoughts?

✠ Purchased, viewed, or made use of pornography?

✠ Watched movies and television that involved sex and nudity?

✠ Listened to music or jokes that were harmful to purity?

✠ Committed adultery? (Sexual relations with someone who is married, or with someone other than my spouse.)

- ✠ Committed incest? (Sexual relations with a relative or in-law.)
- ✠ Committed fornication? (Sexual relations with someone of the opposite sex when neither is married.)
- ✠ Engaged in homosexual activity? (Sexual activity with someone of the same sex.)
- ✠ Committed rape?
- ✠ Masturbated? (Deliberate stimulation of one's own sexual organs for sexual pleasure.)
- ✠ Engaged in sexual foreplay (petting) reserved for marriage?
- ✠ Preyed upon children or youth for my sexual pleasure?
- ✠ Engaged in unnatural sexual activities?
- ✠ Engaged in prostitution, or paid for the services of a prostitute?
- ✠ Seduced someone, or allowed myself to be seduced?
- ✠ Made uninvited and unwelcome sexual advances toward another?
- ✠ Purposely dressed immodestly?

Seventh and Tenth Commandments
**You shall not steal. You shall not covet your
  neighbor's goods.** Have I ...

✠ Stolen? (Take something that doesn't belong to me
  against the reasonable will of the owner.)
✠ Envied others on account of their possessions?
✠ Tried to live in a spirit of Gospel poverty and
  simplicity?
✠ Given generously to others in need?
✠ Considered that God has provided me with money
  so that I might use it to benefit others, as well as
  for my own legitimate needs?
✠ Freed myself from a consumer mentality?
✠ Practiced the works of mercy?
✠ Deliberately defaced, destroyed, or lost another's
  property?
✠ Cheated on a test, taxes, sports, games, or in
  business?
✠ Squandered money in compulsive gambling?
✠ Make a false claim to an insurance company?
✠ Paid my employees a living wage, or failed to give
  a full day's work for a full day's pay?
✠ Failed to honor my part of a contract?
✠ Failed to make good on a debt?
✠ Overcharged someone, especially to take
  advantage of another's hardship or ignorance?
✠ Misused natural resources?

Eighth Commandment
You shall not bear false witness against your neighbor. Have I ...

✠ Lied?

✠ Knowingly and willfully deceived another?

✠ Perjured myself under oath?

✠ Gossiped?

✠ Committed detraction? (Destroying a person's reputation by telling others about his faults for no good reason.)

✠ Committed slander or calumny? (Telling lies about another person in order to destroy his reputation.)

✠ Committed libel? (Writing lies about another person in order to destroy his reputation.)

✠ Been guilty of rash judgment? (Assuming the worst of another person based on circumstantial evidence.)

✠ Failed to make reparation for a lie I told, or for harm done to a person's reputation?

✠ Failed to speak out in defense of the Catholic Faith, the Church, or of another person?

✠ Betrayed another's confidence through speech?

Do not just be a channel for grace,
but a reservoir, an overflowing reservoir.
No sooner has a channel received
grace than it pours it out.
A reservoir waits to be filled up and
then offers grace to those who come to
draw from its superabundance.

St. Bernadette

Stations of the Cross

The following meditations on the Stations of the Cross were written by St. Alphonsus Liguori.

Preparatory Prayer

(To be said kneeling before the altar.)

All: My Lord, Jesus Christ, You have made this journey to die for me with unspeakable love, and I have so many times ungratefully abandoned You. But now I love You with all my heart, and, because I love You, I am sincerely sorry for ever having offended You. Pardon me, my God, and permit me to accompany You on this journey. You go to die for love of me; I want, my beloved Redeemer, to die for love of You. My Jesus, I will live and die always united to You.

At the cross her station keeping, stood the mournful Mother weeping, close to Jesus to the last.

The First Station: Pilate Condemns Jesus to Die

V: We adore You, O Christ, and we praise You. (Genuflect)

R: Because, by Your holy cross, You have redeemed the world. (Rise)

V: Consider how Jesus Christ, after being scourged and crowned with thorns, was unjustly condemned by Pilate to die on the cross. (Kneel)

R: My adorable Jesus, it was not Pilate, no, it was my sins that condemned You to die. I beseech You, by the merits of this sorrowful journey, to assist my soul on its journey to eternity. I love You, beloved Jesus; I love You more than I love myself. With all my heart I repent of ever having offended You. Grant that I may love You always, and then do with me as You will.

(Our Father, Hail Mary, Glory Be.)

Through her heart, His sorrow sharing, all His bitter anguish bearing, now at length the sword has passed.

The Second Station: Jesus Accepts His Cross

V: We adore You, O Christ, and we praise You. (Genuflect)

R: Because, by Your holy cross, You have redeemed the world. (Rise)

V: Consider Jesus as He walked this road with the cross on His shoulders, thinking of us and offering to His Father on our behalf the death He was about to suffer. (Kneel)

R: My most beloved Jesus, I embrace all the sufferings You have destined for me until death. I beg You, by all You suffered in carrying Your cross, to help me carry mine with Your perfect peace and resignation. I love You, Jesus, my love; I repent of ever having offended You. Never let me separate myself from You again. Grant that I may love You always, and then do with me as You will.

(Our Father, Hail Mary, Glory Be.)

O, how sad and sore depressed was that Mother highly blessed of the sole Begotten One.

The Third Station: Jesus Falls the First Time

V: We adore You, O Christ, and we praise You. (Genuflect)

R: Because, by Your holy cross, You have redeemed the world. (Rise)

V: Consider the first fall of Jesus. Loss of blood from the scourging and crowing with thorns had so weakened Him that He could hardly walk, and yet He had to carry that great load upon His shoulders. As the soldiers struck Him cruelly, He fell several times under the heavy cross. (Kneel)

R: My beloved Jesus, it was not the weight of the cross but the weight of my sins which made You suffer so much. By the merits of this first fall, save me from falling into mortal sin. I love You, O my Jesus, with all my heart; I am sorry that I have offended You. May I never offend You again. Grant that I may love You always, and then do with me as You will.

(Our Father, Hail Mary, Glory Be.)

Christ above in torment hangs. She beneath beholds the pangs of her dying, glorious Son.

The Fourth Station: Jesus Meets His Afflicted Mother

V: We adore You, O Christ, and we praise You. (Genuflect)

R: Because, by Your holy cross, You have redeemed the world. (Rise)

V: Consider how the Son met His Mother on His way to Calvary. Jesus and Mary gazed at each other and their looks became as so many arrows to wound those hearts which loved each other so tenderly. (Kneel)

R: My most loving Jesus, by the pain You suffered in this meeting grant me the grace of being truly devoted to Your most holy Mother. And you, my Queen, who was overwhelmed with sorrow, obtain for me by your prayers a tender and a lasting remembrance of the passion of your divine Son. I love You, Jesus, my Love, above all things. I repent of ever having offended You. Never allow me to offend You again. Grant that I may love You always, and then do with me as You will.

(Our Father, Hail Mary, Glory Be.)

Is there one who would not weep, 'whelmed in miseries so deep, Christ's dear Mother to behold.

The Fifth Station: Simon Helps Jesus Carry the Cross

V: We adore You, O Christ, and we praise You. (Genuflect)

R: Because, by Your holy cross, You have redeemed the world. (Rise)

V: Consider how weak and weary Jesus was. At each step He was at the point of expiring. Fearing that He would die on the way when they wished Him to die the infamous death of the cross, they forced Simon of Cyrene to help carry the cross after Our Lord. (Kneel)

R: My beloved Jesus, I will not refuse the cross as Simon did: I accept it and embrace it. I accept in particular the death that is destined for me with all the pains that may accompany it. I unite it to Your death and I offer it to You. You have died for love of me; I will die for love of You and to please You. Help me by Your grace. I love You, Jesus, my love; I repent of ever having offended You. Never let me offend You again. Grant that I may love You always, and then do with me as You will.

(Our Father, Hail Mary, Glory Be.)

Can the human heart refrain from partaking in her pain, in that Mother's pain untold.

The Sixth Station: Veronica Offers Her Veil to Jesus

V: We adore You, O Christ, and we praise You. (Genuflect)

R: Because, by Your holy cross, You have redeemed the world. (Rise)

V: Consider the compassion of the holy woman, Veronica. Seeing Jesus in such distress, His face bathed in sweat and blood, she presented Him with her veil. Jesus wiped His face and left upon the cloth the image of His sacred countenance. (Kneel)

R: My beloved Jesus, Your face was beautiful before You began this journey, but now it no longer appears beautiful and is disfigured with wounds and blood. Alas, my soul also was once beautiful when it received Your grace in Baptism, but I have since disfigured it with my sins. You alone, my Redeemer, can restore it to its former beauty. Do this by the merits of Your passion, and then do with me as You will.

(Our Father, Hail Mary, Glory Be.)

Bruised, derided, cursed, defiled she beheld her tender Child all with bloody scourges rent.

The Seventh Station: Jesus Falls the Second Time

V: We adore You, O Christ, and we praise You. (Genuflect)

R: Because, by Your holy cross, You have redeemed the world. (Rise)

V: Consider how the second fall of Jesus under His cross renews the pain in all the wounds of the head and members of our afflicted Lord. (Kneel)

R: My most gentle Jesus, how many times You have forgiven me; and how many times I have fallen again and begun again to offend You! By the merits of this second fall, give me the grace to persevere in Your love until death. Grant, that in all my temptations, I may always have recourse to You. I love You, Jesus my love, with all my heart; I am sorry that I have offended You. Never let me offend You again. Grant that I may love You always, and then do with me as You will.

(Our Father, Hail Mary, Glory Be.)

For the sins of His own nation saw Him hang in desolation 'til His spirit forth He sent.

The Eighth Station: Jesus Speaks to the Women

V: We adore You, O Christ, and we praise You. (Genuflect)

R: Because, by Your holy cross, You have redeemed the world. (Rise)

V: Consider how the women wept with compassion seeing Jesus so distressed and dripping with blood as He walked along. Jesus said to them, "Weep not so much for me, but rather for Your children." (Kneel)

R: My Jesus, laden with sorrows, I weep for the sins which I have committed against You because of the punishment I deserve for them, and still more because of the displeasure they have caused You, Who have loved me with an infinite love. It is Your love, more than the fear of hell, which makes me weep for my sins. My Jesus, I love You more than myself; I am sorry that I have offended You. Never allow me to offend You again. Grant that I may love You always, and then do with me as You will.

(Our Father, Hail Mary, Glory Be.)

O sweet Mother! Fount of love, touch my spirit from above. Make my heart with yours accord.

The Ninth Station: Jesus Falls the Third Time

V: We adore You, O Christ, and we praise You. (Genuflect)

R: Because, by Your holy cross, You have redeemed the world. (Rise)

V: Consider how Jesus Christ fell for the third time. He was extremely weak and the cruelty of His executioners was excessive; they tried to hasten His steps though He hardly had strength to move. (Kneel)

R: My outraged Jesus, by the weakness You suffered in going to Calvary, give me enough strength to overcome all human respect and all my evil passions which have led me to despise Your friendship. I love You, Jesus my love, with all my heart; I am sorry for ever having offended You. Never permit me to offend You again. Grant that I may love You always, and then do with me as You will.

(Our Father, Hail Mary, Glory Be.)

Make me feel as You have felt. Make my soul to glow and melt with the love of Christ, my Lord.

The Tenth Station: Jesus Is Stripped of His Garments

V: We adore You, O Christ, and we praise You. (Genuflect)

R: Because, by Your holy cross, You have redeemed the world. (Rise)

V: Consider how Jesus was violently stripped of His clothes by His executioners. The inner garments adhered to His lacerated flesh and the soldiers tore them off so roughly that the skin came with them. Have pity for your Savior so cruelly treated and tell Him: (Kneel)

R: My innocent Jesus, by the torment You suffered in being stripped of Your garments, help me to strip myself of all attachment for the things of earth that I may place all my love in You, Who are so worthy of my love. I love You, O Jesus, with all my heart; I am sorry for ever having offended You. Never let me offend You again. Grant that I may love You always, and then do with me as You will.

(Our Father, Hail Mary, Glory Be.)

Holy Mother, pierce me through, in my heart each wound renew of my Savior crucified.

The Eleventh Station: Jesus Is Nailed to the Cross

V: We adore You, O Christ, and we praise You. (Genuflect)

R: Because, by Your holy cross, You have redeemed the world. (Rise)

V: Consider Jesus, thrown down upon the cross: He stretched out His arms and offered to His eternal Father the sacrifice of His life for our salvation. They nailed His hands and feet, and then, raising the cross, left Him to die in anguish. (Kneel)

R: My despised Jesus, nail my heart to the cross that it may always remain there to love You and never leave You again. I love You more than myself; I am sorry for ever having offended You. Never permit me to offend You again. Grant that I may love You always, and then do with me as You will.

(Our Father, Hail Mary, Glory Be.)

Let me share with you His pain, Who for all our sins was slain, Who for me in torments died.

The Twelfth Station: Jesus Dies Upon the Cross

V: We adore You, O Christ, and we praise You. (Genuflect)

R: Because, by Your holy cross, You have redeemed the world. (Rise)

V: Consider how your Jesus, after three hours of agony on the cross, is finally overwhelmed with suffering and, abandoning Himself to the weight of His body, bows His head and dies. (Kneel)

R: My dying Jesus, I devoutly kiss the cross on which You would die for love of me. I deserve, because of my sins, to die a terrible death, but Your death is my hope. By the merits of Your death, give me the grace to die embracing Your feet and burning with love of You. I yield my soul into Your hands. I love You with my whole heart. I am sorry that I have offended You. Never let me offend You again. Grant that I may love You always, and then do with me as You will.

(Our Father, Hail Mary, Glory Be.)

Let me mingle tears with thee, mourning Him Who mourned for me, all the days that I may live.

The Thirteenth Station: Jesus Is Taken Down from the Cross

V: We adore You, O Christ, and we praise You. (Genuflect)

R: Because, by Your holy cross, You have redeemed the world. (Rise)

V: Consider how, after Our Lord had died, He was taken down from the cross by two of His disciples, Joseph and Nicodemus, and placed in the arms of His afflicted Mother. She received Him with unutterable tenderness and pressed Him close to her bosom. (Kneel)

R: O Mother of Sorrows, for the love of Your Son, accept me as Your servant and pray to Him for me. And You, my Redeemer, since You have died for me, allow me to love You, for I desire only You and nothing more. I love You, Jesus my love, and I am sorry that I have offended You. Never let me offend You again. Grant that I may love You always, and then do with me as You will.

(Our Father, Hail Mary, Glory Be.)

By the cross with you to stay, there with you to weep and pray, is all I ask of you to give.

The Fourteenth Station: Jesus Is Placed in the Sepulcher

V: We adore You, O Christ, and we praise You. (Genuflect)

R: Because, by Your holy cross, You have redeemed the world. (Rise)

V: Consider how the disciples carried the body of Jesus to its burial while His holy Mother went with them and arranged it in the sepulcher with her own hands. They then closed the tomb and all departed. (Kneel)

R: Oh, my buried Jesus, I kiss the stone that closes You in. But You gloriously did rise again on the third day. I beg You by Your resurrection that I may be raised gloriously on the last day, to be united with You in heaven, to praise You and love You forever. I love You, Jesus, and I repent of ever having offended You. Grant that I may love You always, and then do with me as You will.

(Our Father, Hail Mary, Glory Be.)

Virgin of all virgins blest! Listen to my fond request: Let me share your grief divine.

Prayer to Jesus Christ Crucified

My good and dear Jesus, I kneel before You, asking You most earnestly to engrave upon my heart a deep and lively faith, hope, and charity, with true repentance for my sins, and a firm resolve to make amends. As I reflect upon Your five wounds and dwell upon them with deep compassion and grief, I recall, good Jesus, the words the Prophet David spoke long ago concerning Yourself: "They pierced My hands and My feet; they have numbered all My bones."

PART TWO

HOLY ALLIANCE

"I've got your six" is a military phrase that basically means "I've got your back." It comes from the old pilot system in which directions correspond to hours on the clock, where 12 o'clock is forward and 6 o'clock is behind. Thus anyone behind you is "at your six."

We are not meant to advance unaided. In His great wisdom, God has set up a Holy Alliance that, once united, is designed to defeat any and all forces of darkness in the heavenly realm, rescue souls, and build up the kingdom of God. This alliance is called the Communion of Saints. It is comprised of the Church Militant (those alive on earth), the Church Penitent (those undergoing purification in purgatory in preparation for heaven), and the Church Triumphant (those already in heaven).

It is the exchange of the *Sancta Sanctis*! ("God's holy gifts for God's holy people!") Those on earth (Church Militant) invoke the saints in heaven and pray for the souls in purgatory (we can gain indulgences for them). When called upon, those in heaven pray for the Church Militant and the Church Penitent; they obtain graces for us on earth and an alleviation of suffering for the poor souls in purgatory. Those in purgatory can, when called upon, invoke the saints on high and pray for us struggling with the world, the flesh, and the evil spirit.

St. Thomas Aquinas wrote: "Charity is incomplete until it includes the dead as well as the living." While we live together on earth as Christians, we are in communion, or unity, with one another. But that communion doesn't end when one of us dies. In the Communion of Saints "a perennial link of charity exists between the faithful who have already reached their heavenly home, those who are expiating their sins in purgatory, and those who are still pilgrims on earth. Between them there is, too, an abundant exchange of all good things."[16] In other words, the bond of love remains, along with the self-emptying nature of that real love. Even separated by death, we continue to care for each other, look out for each other, and build each other up. And so we continue to say to one another, "I've got your six!"

To understand how God's amazing structure for this loving exchange of spiritual goods is built, we must learn what we mean by indulgences. St. Ignatius of Loyola wrote, "Indulgences are of such value that I find myself unable to appreciate them according to their true worth or to speak of them highly enough. Thus I exhort you to hold them in the highest possible esteem."

Indulgences 101

What is an indulgence? The word comes from the Latin *indulgentia*, which means "to be kind or tender." "To understand what an indulgence is," writes contemporary author Steve Kellmeyer, "we have to know what our sin does to the world and ourselves. When we commit sin, two things happen. First, we kill the life of grace within us. This deserves punishment. Spiritually, a sinner is a dead man, walking. Second, by removing grace from ourselves, we also remove grace from the created universe. Thus, each sin, no matter how venial, attacks both the moral order of the universe and the very material of creation itself."[17]

The following explanation of indulgences comes from Steve Kellmeyer's *Calendar of Indulgences*:

> **"Forgiveness:** When God pours out mercy in the Sacrament of Reconciliation, He does something we have no right to expect — He forgives our sins and restores the life of grace within us, resurrecting us from death. As a result, we must act (penance) to change our life and renew our way of living (amendment of life). However, though we have been resurrected, we still deserve punishment for the attack we made on God's creation. Further, the horrible consequences of our attack, which removed grace from creation, continue to affect the world even if we ourselves have been healed through

the sacrament. God expects us to help repair the damage.

"Repair Work: We can do this repair work either here on earth or in purgatory. Since God intended us to live with our bodies united to our souls, it is much easier to do this repair work here. In purgatory, our soul and body are separate. The suffering of purgatory is always much more painful than suffering on earth because it is harder to do the necessary repair work when the body isn't around to help.

"The Storehouse: Cardinal John Newman said, 'The smallest venial sin rocks the foundations of the created world.' That is, even our smallest sin can cause devastating consequences in creation; famine, disease, natural disaster. However, through God's grace, the holiness of even the lowliest saint far exceeds the harm even the greatest sinner can do. Further, Christ's work on the cross is infinitely greater in merit than that of the greatest saint in Christendom, the Blessed Virgin Mary. Thus, the graces won by Christ and the saints are an infinite treasure that can be used to heal the wounds of the world. God intends us to use this treasury — indeed; we could not help wipe out the effects of our sin without the divine treasury God established. *An indulgence, then, applies the graces won by Christ and the saints to the world so as to heal the wounds I caused by my sins.*"[18]

Conditions for obtaining a plenary indulgence:

✠ Do the work while in a state of grace

✠ Receive sacramental Confession within 20 days of the work (several plenary indulgences may be earned per reception)

✠ Receive Eucharistic communion (one plenary indulgence may be earned per reception of Eucharist)

✠ Pray for the pope's intentions (an Our Father and Hail Mary, or other appropriate prayer, is sufficient)

✠ Have no attachment to sin (even venial) — i.e., the Christian makes an act of the will to love God and despise sin.

Conditions for obtaining a partial indulgence:

✠ Do the work while in a state of grace

✠ Have the general intention of earning an indulgence

Obtainable at any time and in any place:

✠ Adoring the Blessed Sacrament for at least 30 min

✠ Devoutly reading Sacred Scripture for at least 30 minutes

✠ Devoutly performing the Stations of the Cross

✠ Reciting the Rosary with members of the family or in a church, oratory, religious community, or pious association

Conditions for all indulgences:

Steve Kellmeyer, in his *Calendar of Indulgences*, summarizes the conditions for all indulgences:[19]

✠ Only baptized persons in a state of grace who generally intend to do so may earn indulgences.

✠ Indulgences cannot be applied to the living, but only to the one doing the work or to the dead.

✠ Only one plenary indulgence per day can be earned (except for prayer at the hour of one's own death).

✠ Several partial indulgences can be earned during the same day.

✠ If only part of a work with a plenary indulgence attached is completed, a partial indulgence still obtains.

✠ If the penance assigned in Confession has indulgences attached, the one work can satisfy both penance and indulgence.

✠ Confessors may commute the work or the conditions if the penitent cannot perform them due to legitimate obstacles.

✠ In groups, indulgenced prayer must be recited by at least one member while the others at least mentally follow the prayer.

✠ If speech/hearing impairments make reciting impossible, mental expression or reading of the prayer is sufficient.

✠ For an indulgence attached to a particular day requiring a church visit, the day begins at noon the day before and ends at midnight.

Obtainable on special days:

✠ January 1st — Pray "Veni, Creator" (page 101)

✠ Each Friday of Lent and Passiontide after Communion — Pray the "Prayer before a Crucifix" (page 102)

✠ Holy Thursday — Pray "Tantum Ergo" (page 103)

✠ Good Friday — Venerate a crucifix

✠ Paschal Vigil — Renew baptismal promises

✠ Feast of Pentecost — Pray "Veni, Creator" (page 101)

✠ Feast of Corpus Christi — Pray "Tantum Ergo" (page 103)

✠ Feast of the Sacred Heart of Jesus — Pray "Most Sweet Jesus" (Act of Reparation) (page 104)

✠ November 1-8 — Visit a cemetery and pray for the departed

✠ November 2 (All Souls Day) — Visit a church or oratory

✠ Feast of Christ the King — Recite publicly "Most Sweet Jesus, Redeemer" (Act of Dedication to Christ the King) (page 106)

✠ December 31 — Recite publicly "Te Deum" (page 107)

Indulgenced Prayers:

Come, Holy Spirit, Creator Blest

(Veni, Creator)

Come, Holy Spirit, Creator blest, and in our souls take up Your rest; Come with Your grace and heavenly aid to fill the hearts which You have made.

O Comforter, to You we cry; O heavenly gift of God Most High; O fount of life and fire of love and sweet anointing from above.

You in Your sevenfold gifts are known; You, finger of God's hand we own; You, promise of the Father, You Who do the tongue with power imbue.

Kindle our senses from above, and make our hearts o'erflow with love; With patience firm and virtue high, the weakness of our flesh supply.

Far from us drive the foe we dread, and grant us Your peace instead; so shall we not, with You for guide, turn from the path of life aside.

Oh, may Your grace on us bestow the Father and the Son to know; And You, through endless times confessed, of both the eternal Spirit blest.

Now to the Father and the Son, Who rose from death, be glory given, with You, O holy Comforter, henceforth by all in earth and heaven. Amen.

Prayer before a Crucifix

Behold, O good and most sweet Jesus, I fall upon my knees before Thee, and with most fervent desire beg and beseech Thee that Thou wouldst impress upon my heart a lively sense of faith, hope, and charity, true repentance for my sins, and a firm resolve to make amends. And with deep affection and grief, I reflect upon Thy five wounds, having before my eyes that which Thy prophet David spoke about Thee, O good Jesus: "They have pierced my hands and feet, they have counted all my bones." Amen.

Crucifix by Segna Di Buonaventure, Siena. Painted in 1310-15 on wood. Currently in the Pinacoteca Nazionale, Siena.

Tantum Ergo (by St. Thomas Aquinas):

Tantum ergo Sacramentum Veneremur cernui: Et antiquum documentum Novo cedat ritui: Praestet fides supplementum Sensuum defectui.

Genitori, Genitoque Laus et jubilatio, Salus, honor, virtus quoque Sit et benedictio: Procedenti ab utroque Compar sit laudatio. Amen.

Down in adoration falling, Lo! the sacred Host we hail, Lo! o'er ancient forms departing, newer rites of grace prevail; Faith for all defects supplying, where the feeble senses fail.

To the everlasting Father, and the Son Who reigns on high, with the Holy Spirit proceeding, forth from each eternally, be salvation, honor, blessing, might, and endless majesty. Amen.

Holy Communion is the shortest and safest way to Heaven.

Pope St. Pius X

Most Sweet Jesus - Act of Reparation

Most sweet Jesus, Whose overflowing charity for men is requited by so much forgetfulness, negligence, and contempt, behold us prostrate before You, eager to repair by a special act of homage the cruel indifference and injuries to which Your loving Heart is everywhere subject.

Mindful, alas! that we ourselves have had a share in such great indignities, which we now deplore from the depths of our hearts, we humbly ask Your pardon and declare our readiness to atone by voluntary expiation, not only for our own personal offenses, but also for the sins of those, who, straying far from the path of salvation, refuse in their obstinate infidelity to follow You, their Shepherd and Leader, or, renouncing the promises of their Baptism, have cast off the sweet yoke of Your law.

We are now resolved to expiate each and every deplorable outrage committed against You; we are now determined to make amends for the manifold offenses against Christian modesty in unbecoming dress and behavior, for all the foul seductions laid to ensnare the feet of the innocent, for the frequent violations of Sundays and holy-days, and the shocking blasphemies uttered against You and Your saints. We wish also to make amends for the insults to which Your vicar on earth and Your priests are subjected, for the profanation, by conscious neglect or terrible acts of sacrilege, of the very Sacrament of

Your divine love, and lastly for the public crimes of nations who resist the rights and teaching authority of the Church which You have founded.

Would that we were able to wash away such abominations with our blood. We now offer, in reparation for these violations of Your divine honor, the satisfaction You once made to Your Eternal Father on the cross and which You continue to renew daily on our altars; we offer it in union with the acts of atonement of Your Virgin Mother and all the saints and of the pious faithful on earth; and we sincerely promise to make recompense, as far as we can with the help of Your grace, for all neglect of Your great love and for the sins we and others have committed in the past. Henceforth, we will live a life of unswerving faith, of purity of conduct, of perfect observance of the precepts of the Gospel, and especially that of charity. We promise to the best of our power to prevent others from offending You and to bring as many as possible to follow You.

O loving Jesus, through the intercession of the Blessed Virgin Mother, our model in reparation, deign to receive the voluntary offering we make of this act of expiation; and by the crowning gift of perseverance keep us faithful unto death in our duty and the allegiance we owe to You, so that we may all one day come to that happy home, where with the Father and the Holy Spirit You live and reign, God, forever and ever. Amen.

Most Sweet Jesus, Redeemer - Act of Dedication to Christ the King (Pope Pius XI)

Most Sweet Jesus, Redeemer of the human race, look down upon us humbly prostrate before You. We are Yours, and Yours we wish to be; but to be more surely united with You, behold each one of us freely consecrates himself today to Your Most Sacred Heart. Many indeed have never known You; many, too, despising Your precepts, have rejected You. Have mercy on them all, most merciful Jesus, and draw them to Your Sacred Heart.

Be King, O Lord, not only of the faithful who have never forsaken You, but also of the prodigal children who have abandoned You; grant that they may quickly return to their Father's house, lest they die of wretchedness and hunger.

Be King of those who are deceived by erroneous opinions, or whom discord keeps aloof, and call them back to the harbor of Truth and the unity of Faith, so that soon there may be but one flock and one Shepherd.

Grant, O Lord, to Your Church assurance of freedom and immunity from harm; give tranquility of order to all nations; make the earth resound from pole to pole with one cry: Praise to the Divine Heart that wrought our salvation; to It be glory and honor forever. Amen.

Te Deum

O God, we praise You and acknowledge You to be the Supreme Lord. Everlasting Father, all the earth worships You. All the angels, the heavens, and all angelic powers, all the cherubim and seraphim continuously cry to You: Holy, holy, holy, Lord, God of Hosts! Heaven and earth are full of the majesty of Your glory.

The glorious choir of the apostles, the wonderful company of prophets, the white-robed army of martyrs praise You. Holy Church throughout the world acknowledges You: The Father of infinite majesty; Your adorable, true, and only Son; also the Holy Spirit, the Comforter.

O Christ, You are the King of glory! You are the everlasting Son of the Father. When You took it upon Yourself to deliver man, You did not disdain the Virgin's womb. Having overcome the sting of death, You opened the kingdom of heaven to all believers. You sit at the right hand of God in the glory of the Father.

We believe that You will come to be our Judge. We, therefore, beg You to help Your servants whom You have redeemed with Your Precious Blood. Let them be numbered with Your saints in everlasting glory. Save Your people, O Lord, and bless Your inheritance! Govern them, and raise them up forever.

Every day we thank You. And we praise Your name forever; yes, forever and ever. O Lord, deign to keep us from sin this day. Have mercy on us, O Lord, have mercy on us. Let Your mercy, O Lord, be upon us, for we have hoped in You. O Lord, in You I have put my trust; let me never be put to shame.

You know well enough that
Our Lord does not look so much at the
greatness of our actions,
nor even at their difficulty,
but at the love with which
we do them.

St. Therese of Lisieux

CITATIONS

[1] Barron, Fr. Robert. Sermon 522, "Priest, Prophet, and King." The Baptism of the Lord. <http://www.wordonfire.org/WOF-Radio/Sermons/Sermon-Archive-for-2011/Sermon-522---Priest,-Prophet,-and-King---The-Bapti.aspx> Accessed 8 May 2012.

[2] Hartch, Todd. "Born for Combat," The Catholic Thing, 3 February 2011. Quoting and paraphrasing Pope Leo XIII's Sapientiae Christianae. <http://www.thecatholicthing.org/columns/2011/born-for-combat.html> Accessed 8 May 2012.

[3] Chautard, Jean-Baptiste. Soul of the Apostolate. Part 4, Section F.

[4] St. Josemaria Escriva, The Way. Chapter 28, Number 629.

[5] McCloskey, Fr. John, "The Seven Daily Habits of Holy Apostolic People," CatholiCity. <http://www.catholicity.com/mccloskey/sevenhabits.html> Accessed 9 May 2012.

[6] Ibid.

[7] St. Josemaria Escriva, The Way, Chapter 6, Number 191.

[8] St. Josemaria Escriva, The Way, Chapter 3, Number 116.

[9] St. Josemaria Escriva, Furrow, Chapter 14, Number 474.

[10] McCloskey, Fr. John, Ibid.

[11] Philippe, Fr. Jacques. Time for God. Scepter Publishers, 2008.

[12] St. Josemaria Escriva, The Way, Chapter 3, Number 91.

[13] Tucciarone, Tracy. "Lectio Divina," Fish Eaters. <http://www.fisheaters.com/lectiodivina.html> Accessed 9 May 2012.

[14] Socias, Fr. James, ed. Handbook of Prayers. Midwest Theological Forum, Woodridge, Ill., 2007.

[15] "A Detailed Catholic Examination of Conscience," Beginning Catholic, <http://www.beginningcatholic.com/catholic-examination-of-conscience.html> Accessed 9 May 2012.

[16] Pope Paul VI, Indulgentiarum doctrina, Apostolic Constitution, Chapter 2, Number 5.

[17] Kellmeyer, Steve, The Beauty of Grace Calendar of Indulgences 2012, Bridegroom Press, Plano, Texas, 2012. Available through BridegroomPress.com.

[18] Ibid.

[19] Ibid.